This book is published strictly for historical purposes. The Naval and Military Press Ltd expressly bears no responsibility or liability of any type, to any first, second or third party, for any harm, injury or loss whatsoever.

AMERICAN JUDO

By

Arthur Hobart Farrar
Author of "Police Jiu-Jitsu"

A Manual of Kodokwan Judo, thoroughly modernized and particularly adapted for use in our Armed Forces.

Engagingly told lessons in the Art of Hand-to-Hand Combat; rugged with the strength and spirit of American Manhood and Womanhood.

The Naval & Military Press Ltd

Published by

The Naval & Military Press Ltd
Unit 5 Riverside, Brambleside
Bellbrook Industrial Estate
Uckfield, East Sussex
TN22 1QQ England

Tel: +44 (0)1825 749494

www.naval-military-press.com
www.nmarchive.com

In reprinting in facsimile from the original, any imperfections are inevitably reproduced and the quality may fall short of modern type and cartographic standards.

TABLE OF CONTENTS

	Page
Foreword	5
What is Judo?	7
Thumb-Wrist-Elbow-Shoulder Break	9
Leg-Assist	12
Crotch-Teeter Break	14
Shoulder-Arm Fulcrum Break	17
Wrist Hold Breach	21
Thumb Grasp Wrist Breach	24
Wrist Breach and Knee Attack	27
Rear Waist Breach	31
Circus Mule Trick	34
Modified Flying-Mare	37
Arm Pinion	40
Knife Counter	44
Strangle Hold	49
Straddle Choke	53
Bent-Arm Straddle Choke	56
Strangle Breach	60
Strangle-Breach by "Push"	63
Body-Blow of Solar Plexus Punch	63
Double-Knuckle Screw	66
Upward Battering-Ram	67
Strangle Breach Follow-Up	69
Hair-Pull and Punishment	74
Punch-Throw Counter	78
Punch-Throw (continued)	81
Crotch-Kick Counter	83
Waist Breach	86

FOREWORD

It is most unfortunate, for the peace of man's soul and the joy of his body that the leaders of men so corrupt the good works of each century or generation, that the good that is in all mankind is turned against him.

There is a yearning in every race, be it savage or civilized (so-called), that transcends the urgings of the professional racialist and which drives the individual and his social counterpart, the Nation, to establish a basic ethical conduct for the uplift of all. Such a yearning brought about Judo, with its knightly standards designed to foster the spirit of fair-play and develop a sane and honest mind in a healthy body.

In the Japan of today, with its brutal war lords possessing the body and soul of the Japanese people, all the concentrated fury of evil men has been inculcated in the minds of its little, brown men, whom we have once admired. They were once the subject of great homilies and eulogies by the civilized world, who are now social pariahs and outcasts among decent peoples of the world, for all the three hundred years of teaching of Bushido has been abandoned in a decade to gratify the ambitions of ruthless barons determined to rule the world or ruin their own nation and all others with whom they come in contact, either by fair means or foul. The rape of a race akin to their own, the Chinese, but who are infinitely older in civilization, has aroused the hatred of all freedom-loving peoples of the earth and has kindled an undying determination to destroy the power they have seized and to pay them in coin for their ruthless emulation of all that was evil and sadistic in Occidental society.

Nevertheless, when the smoke of battle will lift, and the living have counted their costs, mourned their dead and punished the atavisms that have attempted to rule a Globe, if there is one thing that will stand out and remain as a monument to the Japanese Nation, it will be Judo that will be remembered.

While the depredations of the Japanese War Lords are still fresh in our minds and our scorn for their misuse of this once noble Art and Science of a great people is still burning in us, it is more than wise to know what Judo is and how we may utilize its teachings for the uplift of our own physical well-being and ironically use their own weapons against them.

Foolish it would be indeed, for us, to sneer at everything an enemy possesses. Criminal, if we cannot learn from a foe how to "blast" him with his own weapon. If Judo is good for the Japanese then it is doubly good for Americans to use against the Nipponese. It is a sort of retributive justice for us to learn what they know and then confound them with that knowledge.

It is, therefore, the hope of the writer that this Art and Science of Judo will be learned with that thought in view, with the spirit — the offensive spirit — if you will, of considering Judo as a "Big Gun" cast and molded in Japan and trained against Hirohito and his cowardly assassins to their destruction.

"Judo for Americans" will not extol the virtues of Bushido, or throw any halos around the "strong" men of Nippon nor dwell on the wiliness of the little heathens, but will dwell sometimes in a most uncomplimentary fashion on the "vermin" nations of the world and endeavor to show how to overcome "Herrenvolk" and supermen alike as individuals. The world we live in is beginning to realize the dignity and value of the individual and is sick to its collective stomach with the mass mind and the mass subservience. The conflict now rampant emphasizes the worth of each man and consequently Judo, the contest between man and man, is just the kind of a physical and mental training which will bring out the merit of man.

That shall be our task in this book.

Author

WHAT IS JUDO?

Let us say at the outset that Judo is the improved, modernized form of the most ancient sport and science known to all of us as Jiu-Jitsu. It was variously known as Taijitsu or Judo, but has latterly, due to its use by the Commando regiments of England and the Rangers of America, and the very simplicity and euphony of its name, come to be generally called JUDO.

Jiu-Jitsu, itself, was originally a military art in old Japan before the days of Perry. It has been practiced there for three hundred years.

While, from time to time, weapons were used and woven into the texture of the art of Jiu-Jitsu, mainly it was the art of controlling or overcoming, with the naked hands, enemies of the nation or of the state, such as criminals. It was therefore, the Police, that in peace times, were principally taught Jiu-Jitsu. The Nipponese police called it by the name of Torite or the art of arresting. But since it was and is a system of offense as well as defense, it was quickly utilized by the military in their training of recruits.

Jiu-Jitsu, however, had no "spiritual" content at all. It had no ethical standards. It broke all the rules of physical culture and sacrificed body-building to the strain of contest.

Judo, however, crystallized all the best that was in Jiu-Jitsu, freed the science from all ridiculous posturings, silly "mugging" so often seen in Japanese contests of strength, and combined training and body building with the old holds and tricks, establishing a fine scientific new sport which "paid off" in increased efficiency of body and mind.

The principles of Judo do not depend on violent straining, pulling and tugging, sweating and swearing, but on the utilization of the exertion of an opponent to his own undoing. Since it is primarily not established for the over-strong of body, but for the every-day, normal person, any one may learn it and everyone may practice it. It is barred to no sex nor to any age. Old and young may profit by it.

Judo requires no particular form of training. That is, no strict regimen of diet or gymnastics need be undertaken. If one, consciously does those things that will strengthen his fingers, his hands, wrists, legs, toes, chest and abdominal muscles, no matter how he does it, he is furthering his study of Judo. All he need do, in addition, is to learn some of the very simple rules governing holds and tricks, as set forth in word and picture in this little work, and he should have a working knowledge of Judo.

THUMB-WRIST--ELBOW-SHOULDER BREAK

"Look," said Private First Class Zsimanski, fresh out of Hamtramck — and fresh — to his buddy, Corporal Pinsky from wild and woolly Brooklyn, "this Judo gives me a pain where I sit. I ain't never needed no dirty Jap tricks to down a guy. Two drinks under me belt, and I lifts me fist. Socko and the guy is down — and for the count."

"Sure, and the guy musta been unconscious before you hit him," answered Corp. Pinsky. "What was he doin' when you hit him? Posin'."

"Kiddin' aside," retorted Zsimanski, "I can't seem to get the hang of that thumb-wrist-elbow-shoulder hold. It's got me down. I bet you ain't no better off than me."

"Well, it seems simple to me. With that hold even a little fellow can put a big guy hors de combat."

"What's a horse got to do with it?" said Zsimanski, purple with anger. "You don't mean to say a little pipsqueak like you can actually do something to the likes of me with that Judo?"

"Sure, you big lug," said Pinsky, just a tiny bit peeved by the other's choler. "Want me to try And I ain't talking about horses. Hors de combat means out of action in some foreign language. I picked it up from the Looey."

"Just you face me," continued little Pinsky.

He stood facing Zsimanski a minute or two.

Then he stepped forward. The other, uncertainly stood his ground, his hands held loosely at his side, both hands dangling toward the ground.

Pinsky put his left foot forward and quickly grabbed Zsimanski's right hand, curling his fingers around the other's thumb, his own thumb pressing into the back of the big Private's hand.

With another quick motion he lifted his arm with the captured hand still tightly gripped in his, stepped forward and to his opponent's right.

Pinsky bent at the waist, bringing his right shoulder against the chest and right shoulder of Zsimanski.

He then seized the Private's right hand with his own right hand, curling his fingers into the palm of the other's hand and pressing his right thumb into the back of the captured hand.

With both hands he began to press the captive hand backwards. His elbow kept pressing into the other's chest and his shoulder continued pressing against the other's shoulder.

"Ouch," Zsimanski bellowed. "You're breaking me hand."

"Certainly," laughed Pinsky, "Aint that what the Looey told us? All I have to do is keep pressing a little harder and I'll snap your wrist in two."

"You and who else?" asked Hamtramck's finest, with tears in his eyes. "Let up you runt. I give up."

"Say," he said admiringly, "You catch on fast, don't you. Let's do it again, but slowly, and then I'll try it on you."

"Sure, sure," said the other warily, "we'll do it again— and slowly, but I'm doing it, not you. With this hold and with your strength I'd look like a broken piccolo."

Well, this is what the corporal meant by the thumb-wrist-elbow-shoulder break. A picture will help us to understand what was done.

LEG ASSIST

"Now, Corp." said Pfc. Zsimanski, "this new unit of our's got something with that Judo. But there's somethin' on me mind that keeps me from goin' nuts about it."

"Don't tell me you're going critical on me, me lad," returned the Corporal sarcastically. "First you know nothing about it and now you're getting birth-pangs with an idea."

"You and your high school education," retorted the Pfc. bitterly. "I read a book once too. But I aint braggin'. What I really want to know," he continued earnestly, "is something you forgot to explain the other day. You was tellin' me about that Thumb-wrist-elbow-shoulder break, and I admit you darn near busted me wrist. But even if you was to bust it, what couldn't I do to you with my other hand?"

"Now you got something," said the Coporal. "But you overlooked one thing more the Looey was telling us."

A look of bewilderment came over Zsimanki's face.

"Somethin' else forgot?"

"Yes. You remember you were facing me, and your arms were down by your side. I grabbed your right hand with my left hand squeezing your thumb, my fingers curled around your hand, my thumb digging into the back of your hand."

Let's do it again. See.

Now I bend forward, with my shoulder against your right shoulder, but I step to my left and stretch your arm up and outward, stiff-like. Then I bring my right hand over and grab your hand below your thumb with my right hand and dig my fingers into your palm. Whereupon I bend your hand upwards and inwards at the wrist."

"Sure, I remember all that," said Zsimanski, impatiently, "and don't you be goin' on to break my wrist, you scut. But look, my left hand is free. What's to prevent me from sockin' you one on the beezer?"

"But," laughed the other, "haven't you noticed that when

I stepped to my left, I brought my right foot in front of the inside of your right leg at the knee?"

"Well, what of it?"

"Just this, you numbskull. I just lift my foot a little and kick back at the inside of your knee-joint, like this."

A ludicrous expression came over Zsimanski's face. He felt his right leg give way and before he could balance himself he was down on the ground.

With a swift motion, the corporal, who had released his hand now sank to his right knee on the big Private's right hip, and small as he was, he kept him imprisoned there.

"Now," said he, "that's what the Looey called the Leg-assist. After you have done the thumb-wrist-elbow-shoulder break and have your opponent worrying about the pain in his wrist and whether you will soon break it or not, you can assist his downfall with the kick I just showed you. He won't expect it and the suddenness of your attack will take him off-guard and off-balance.

CROTCH-TEETER BREAK

"Boys," said solemn-faced Lieut. Boyd, in his best professorial manner, "you aren't always going to have the opportunity of facing your opponent with your gun in hand and firing at him from a safe distance."

There was a twinkle in his steel-gray eyes. "You know," he continued, "I used to teach a Y.M.C.A. gym class at home and it was so easy to ask the boys there to be gentlemanly about their bouts. The worst that could happen to any of them was to find themselves dumped on a mat, just a tiny bit woozy. But our friends the Master-folk," his eyes became ominous steel slits and his voice took a hard turn, "aren't playing potsies. The Japs, when you meet them, will hardly hiss politely — so sorree, honorable sor. They'll grab and stab and kick and scratch — if you let them and apologize when the war is over. So let's forget politeness.

"We'll try the hold I'll call the Crotch-Teeter Break. Maybe that isn't what teachers of Judo would call it, but this is Judo for Americans and devil take the Japs.

"You, Jensen," he shouted, pointing at a tall Minnesota Swede, whose corn-silk cow-lick hung loosely over one eye, a-la-Hitler. "Come here."

"Stand, facing me, with your arms down at your side."

Jensen lounged awkwardly forward and stood with his face towards the Lieutenant.

Lieut. Boyd stepped forward until he was almost on top of Jensen, who towered over the C. O. like a hayrick over a mole-hill.

"Watch it, boys," he shouted. "This is important. When I'm through I want you all to pair off. Choose an opponent. Don't look for your best friend. Maybe when it's over you won't have any anyhow."

The Lieutenant reached over across Jensen's chest with his left arm, grasped the other's left coat-lapel firmly with iron fingers, thrusting his forearm under Jensen's chin and gouging his Adam's apple with it.

All this time the Lieut.'s body was slightly to the left of in front of Jensen's big hulk.

Then he bent slightly at the waist, still holding on tightly to the imprisoned lapel—and inserted his right hand in between the legs of Jensen under his crotch.

He bent further until his forearm protruded in back and beyond the other's buttocks, and then reached up until he felt the big Swede's belt, which he thereupon curled his fingers around and held tightly.

Thereupon, with a lightning movement, he pulled on the back of Jensen's belt and heaved him off his feet. Jensen's legs went up into the air. He was held suspended as if he were a big sack of flour.

Lieut. Boyd raised his arms, his right one now bent at the elbow and began to swing or teeter Jensen as if he were a log.

Then, with one mighty effort he brought the big Swede down on the bent knee of his left leg, as if he were breaking a faggot in two.

Jensen groaned and the whole company snickered.

"Aw, Lieut." he whined, "you're killing me."

Lieut. Boyd laughed gratingly.

"Son, you ain't seen nothin' yet."

Having seemingly cracked the other's spine across his bent knee, Lieut. Boyd, then lifted him upward and brought him down with a thump that jarred Jensen's wisdom teeth.

And then to top it all, he dropped on the prone body with his right knee in the other's groin holding him pinned there.

"Now, boys," he said in a business-like manner. "Pair off, like I told you. We haven't any time to listen to Jensen's howls. I'll give him a chance to do the same to me—if he can. And he can—that is, after he tries it a number of times."

Let's get down what he had demonstrated in a graphic illustration.

SHOULDER-ARM FULCRUM BREAK

"I have the honor, men," said the Colonel, "to introduce Major Sanborne, just back from Shanghai. He isn't here to tell you about Jap atrocities. Your newspapers have given you enough of that. But he knows the Japs from way back. He was British military observer in Tokyo some years ago and he learned Judo from some of their experts. He's taught and fought in almost every theater of war and he wants to show you one or two tricks he's learned. Major Sanborne, the field is yours."

The Major was a dapper little man, holding a little swagger stick in his right hand. His peeked cap was at a jaunty slant and he looked as though he had just come out of a band-box. H didn't look like a fighting man.

"Looks like a Limey rooster," muttered Private Hatfield, whose life had been spent, all nineteen years of it, in the saddle where men wear chaps and chaps are bow-legged. "Caint learn much from a bantam."

"Oh, yeah," said Mugs O'Toole out of the side of his mouth. He'd been a bantam fighter from Tenth Avenue. "Many's de guy loined better after I hit 'em. Some o' dem is still scrapin' rosin off deir mushes."

"Quiet," stage-whispered Sgt. Dooley, "or it's latrine detail for youse guys."

Major Sanborne smiled knowingly but took no notice of this behind-the-scenes colloquy.

"I want to show you a little trick the sons of the Rising Sun think only they know," he said in a high-pitched voice. The Rangers snickered silently. This man a fighter!

"I'll need a tall man to assist me," he went on smilingly. "A really big fellow. You, there," he pointed at Private Hatfield. "You're about six something, aren't you?"

"Yes, suh," said Hatfield, sheepishly. "Six, three."

The bantam Major then faced Hatfield and sized him up and down. Hatfield's neck got red.

Without a word the Major took one step forward; advanced his right foot a pace and a bit to the right of Hatfield.

As Hatfield stood uncertainly, with his right hand at his side, the Major suddenly grasped his right wrist with the fingers of his left hand, and the soldier marvelled, while he winced, at the strength and force of that grip.

With the same motion that he used in grabbing Hatfield's hand, the Major pushed the hand he held in his forward and toward the soldier's rear.

He bent slightly at the waist; bent his right knee while his left foot was extended far in back of him to give him a firm footing.

Then with uncanny speed, he reached over, across Hatfield's captured arm until the latter's bicep was nestled under his own arm-pit, and under that captive arm he reached across further and grasped his own left wrist with the fingers of his right hand.

We may pause at this point to paint a real picture by line drawings to show just the kind of hold he had on Private Hatfield:

Had he stopped here alone, the Major would nevertheless have been able to hold the big private a prisoner, but it was evident to all that Hatfield, with his immense strength might well have extricated himself by main force.

However, they were electrified to note that the action was not over.

With a rapid upward movement of both his arms, the Major, putting a good deal of strength and snap to his arms, brought Hatfield's arm up with a galvanic jerk.

There was a sharp outcry and an audible click as if something had broken.

Private Hatfield's face was white and drawn. He was undoubtedly suffering very badly.

Major Sanborne was not smiling.

He grabbed Hatfield's arm and gave it a quick twist and from the momentary gasp of pain and then the look of relief, it was plain that the Major had, by his Shoulder-Arm-Fulcrum break, dislocated Hatfield's arm at the shoulder, and had then put the shoulder back into place.

"I must apologize, Private," the Major said in his peculiar piping voice. "I know I was unnecessarily rough, but I could not demonstrate the hold properly unless I carried through to some degree."

Hatfield, who was the kind of person who admired cleverness in others, did not appear resentful.

"You mean, Major, Sir," he wondered, rubbing his shoulder ruefully, "that you could have done something worse than dislocate my ahm, Sir?"

"Oh, yes," the Major said, "but you wouldn't want me to try it again, would you?"

"No, no," said the other hastily.

"Well," said the Major, "if you wish, I'll show you by merely taking the hold slowly, all over again, this time without any force, you just relaxing and letting me secure the hold without resistance."

He did just that and when he got to the point where he had the arm pinioned under his under-arm, he stopped.

"From now on," he said, "you will note, please that I can do one of two things. Either I can snap up your arm as I did before and dislocate your shoulder; or, if you watch closely and note the fact that I am holding your forearm over my right forearm, all I need do is yank your forearm over the fulcrum made by my arm, applying the force of the pull with my left hand on your wrist. Your forearm would break and snap like a twig."

The look of incredulity passed from Hatfield's face. He looked down on his captured arm and saw that the Major could indeed have broken his arm, using his own right forearm as a fulcrum.

The boys all cheered.

"Well, what d'ye know about that?" muttered little O'Toole, "ain't I always said it's the little guys wid brains that's got the upper hand? That Judo is sumpin'."

Below we give you the (successive steps necessary to carry out the full) action:

WRIST HOLD BREACH

"Hey, Corp.," asked Zsimansky of his side-kick Pinsky, "how'd you like that movie we seen last night at the U. S. O. Canteen?"

"Fair to middlin'," answered the corporal, indifferently.

"You mean you didn't notice nuthin' funny about that pitcher " wondered the other.

"Funny? It was tragic. Boy gets girl. Girl gets ideas. Boy goes west. Girl goes nuts. Boy gets rich, girls gets poor. Poor chump goes east, punches boy friend's nose. Boy gets girl. Multiply that by three thousand and you have every movie in the world, or almost."

"Yeah, you're as funny as a crutch. But did you notice who done the fightin'?"

"Why, Quentin Quibble, of course. Who don't know that ham?"

"Sure, but he's here in Camp?"

"Quentin Quibble?"

"Sure. But he ain't called that. He's just plain Joe Dokes from Oshkosh. He's a buck private like me."

"Well, well, well, what d'ye know?" chuckled Pinsky. "And I suppose you've been pickin' on him ever since you found out."

"Well," said the other slowly, "I sorta tried to, but I take my hat off to the guy. You know he ain't such a bum in this outfit. I always thought he was three-quarters bluff and the balance bull. But I was wrong."

"You mean he's actually got something?"

"Yeah, and how," said Zsimanski, wonderingly. "You know, he learned Judo in college, he says. And I believe him."

"Why?"

"Well, you know the other day I thought I'd have some fun, so I asked him if I could try a hold on him."

"I wasn't suspectin' nuthin'. I just faced him and when I thought he wasn't lookin' I snuck up on him and grabbed his right hand with the fingers of me left hand. I curled

21

me fingers around his wrist, pressing the inside of the wrist with all my might and digging my thumb into the wrist."

"I was just gonna twist his arm and pull it in back of him as you showed me the other day, when all of a sudden I seen him ball his fist, push his elbow up against his own right side and twist his fist inward toward his chest.

"I pressed harder, but before I knew anything, he pulled his arm into his side, then swung his arm upward and with the same quick motion he pushed outward and away from himself.

"He done it so quickly that I felt me fingers give way and was I surprised to find his wrist free. Gee, I thought I was a strong guy. But he's stronger than me."

"Well," said Pinsky, "it may be an accident, but I think the feller has learned Judo somewheres. Look, let's try that hold. You grasp my wrists. Both of them, with your left hand grabbing my right wrist and your right hand grabbing my left wrist."

"Sure. I got it. So what?"

"All right. Now watch closely. I am going to do this slowly so you can see it clearly.

"I twist both my wrists inward, pushing my arms, bent at the elbows against my sides. Like this. Then I ball my fists and twist the balled fists inwards towards my chest.

"Then I pull my arms upwards, and then with force I push my arms outwards, pressing with all my might against your thumbs. You see, the force of my sudden pull upward, my twist inward and the rapid push outwards releases your thumb grips, so that you have to let go."

Zsimanski wasn't exactly astonished. He had seen it demonstrated by Quentin Quibble, but nonetheless he was awed by the little corporal's dexterity.

"Say, you know, you ought to make a diagram of those movements of yours, so I can study them by myself."

"Not a bad idea. I'm not much of an artist, but even a crude line drawing will give you a good idea. Here it is." He drew the following picture of the action:

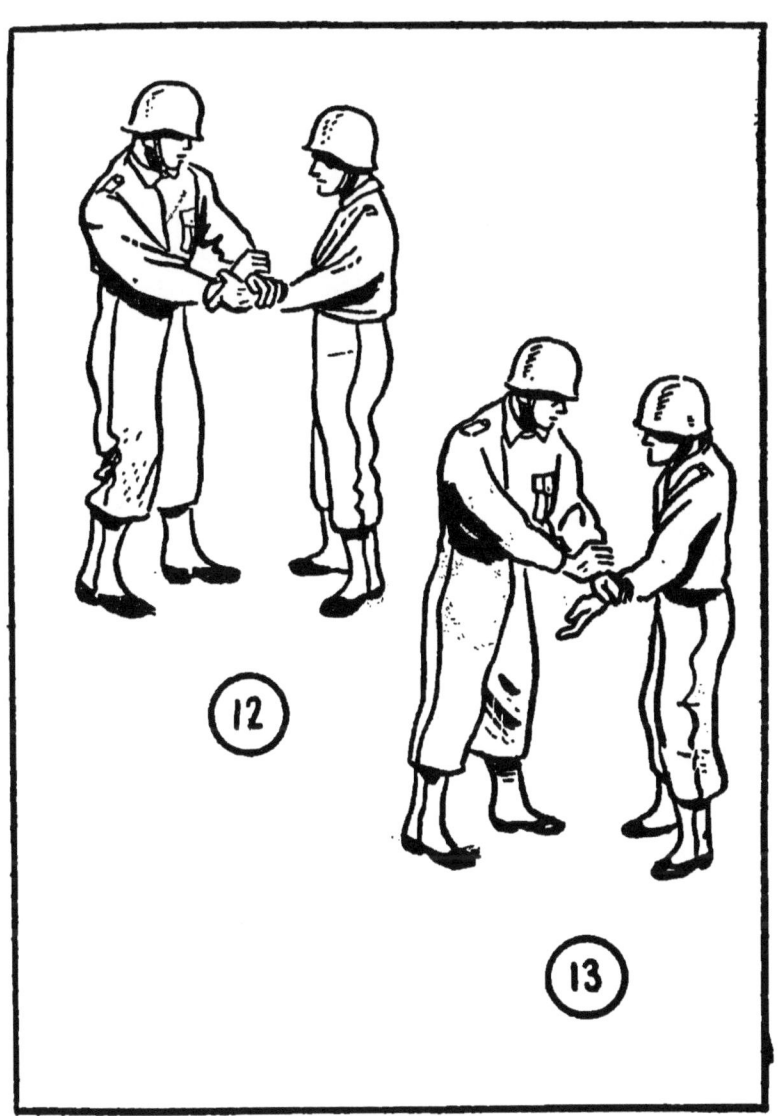

THUMB GRASP WRIST BREACH

"Now, I'm gonna show you sumpin, Pin," said Zsim triumphantly. "You're one of them guys what get's a thing fast, but you ain't got no patent on smartness."

"Well," said Pinsky modestly, "I imagined there were one or two parties knew almost as much as I, but I never dreamed one of them was you."

"Oh, yeah!" sneered Zsimanski. "Lieut. Boyd showed me the trick private like and I tried it on me girl friend, on me furlough. Am I got an in now! Oh, boy!"

"You don't say? Most guys are satisfied to wrestle with their dames in the good old American way, but you got to try Judo to make good. All right, spoofin' aside, let's have it."

"All right, pal, you grab my right wrist with your left hand, see."

The corporal extended his fingers while he faced Zsimanski, and twined them around the latter's left wrist.

"So I got your wrist! So what?" jeered the corporal.

"So this what," panted Zsim.

He moved much more swiftly than the corporal had ever known he could. He then seized the corporal's left wrist with the fingers of his left hand, right below the base of his thumb.

While he was thus holding the corporal's left wrist captive, he suddenly reached across his own left wrist with the fingers of his captured right hand.

With a speed he had never done any kitchen police, he pushed forcefully outward with the hand he held on the corporal's left wrist and at the same time he twisted titanically with his own right wrist against the corporal's thumb which had held his left wrist captive.

The force of the combined pressure outward of Zsim's left hand and the twist of the imprisoned wrist against the corporal's thumb compelled the other's hand to give way. The pain was excruciating and the hold he had was untenable.

This was what it looked like:

"Say," said the corporal with real admiration, "you must have studied hard, all right, to get it down so pat."

"Naw," deprecated Zsimanski, "it comes easy to me. I was thinkin' and thinkin' about it all night and then when I seen Maimie it come to me all of a sudden I could show her sumpin' she ain't never seen before. Was she surprised!"

"So you made the dame, eh?"

"Well, she gave me a kinda slap on the snoot," he replied a little shamefacedly. "But," he added hastily, "if it hadn't a been for her brother who's a cop, she woulda made another date with me."

"You mean you didn't date her up again?"

"Naw, her brother said 'Scram, soldier.' He thought I was wrestlin' with his sister. He's got a mean eye."

"So you tried Judo on him?"

"Naw, I scrammed."

WRIST BREACH AND KNEE ATTACK

This was field maneuvers and the Ranger company were told they would have to make the games realistic.

Lieut. Boyd had warned the boys that on their ability to dish it out as well as take it, might, in real war, depend their very lives. Aside from the fact that being captured would put the company to shame, success in using the holds they had learned might bring the gang a citation from the Colonel.

"And you know what that means " glowed the Lieut.

"Yeah," whispered O'Toole, "a chancet tuh take a coupla days off to send me mudder me laundry for washin'."

"Silence in the ranks," roared the Lieutenant. He pretended not to hear the faint Bronx cheer which went up somewheres in the middle of the company. They were just big, good-natured children.

The night was dark and the Company deployed on the road behind the lumbering tanks which made the air hideous with their clangor.

Somehow Private Zsimanski became detached from the command. He had bent down to tie a loosened shoe-lace. It had taken him longer than he expected in the dark and his Tommy-gun slung heavily across his shoulder.

He thought he heard the marching feet of his comrades, but the shuffling feet he heard seemed to come towards him instead of receding.

Suddenly he felt his wrists seized in a pair of powerful hands.

A voice grated in his ear and a heavy breath was blown into his face. "I got you. Give up?"

He started to tussle but the hold on his wrists grew more imperative, the pressure greater.

And then overhead a flare burst and the road grew as bright as daylight.

He was in the hold of a huge gorilla of a man. It was an American soldier but not one from his Company.

He saw the leer on the other's face and for a moment he was dazed. All the instructions he had received seemed for the moment to desert him. And then he remembered the Lieut.'s words: "Whatever you do, don't get yourselves captured. It will give us a black eye."

"Why," he thought, "here's me chance to prove I know that wrist-breach-knee attack the Lieut. was teachin' us."

And he suited action to words.

Zsim bent both his elbows so that his forearms were pointing upwards. Then with a quick snap in the same direction, his wrists shot up in the air carrying the other's arms upward.

Jubilantly he felt the other's hold on his wrists give way.

Before his opponent got over his astonishment, Zsim grasped the other's wrists in his own hands, but released the others' right wrist almost immediately.

With the same motion he lifted the other's left arm high above his shoulder; brought his own left hand over the back of his opponent's left hand, pressing his own fingers into the palm of the other soldier's hand. He continued the action by bringing his own right hand into play and grabbing the other's left wrist.

With the force of both hands against the left wrist and arm of the other, he bent the wrist backwards and like a bolt out of the blue he lifted his knee, bent at the joint, and brought it in under the crotch of the other.

With the speed of desperation he pivoted on the ball of his right foot and bent his body to his own left. The amazed soldier who opposed him found himself flying downward to the ground.

The force of the pressure against his left wrist and arm and the combined movement of Zaimanski's knee under his crotch, with its agonizing gouging, made him unable to retaliate or even to plan a defense.

Without giving the other a chance to make up his mind, Zsimanski sank down on the stomach of the prone soldier.

"Well done, soldier," he heard a voice say. "He's your prisoner. You may let him up."

Such had been Zsimanski's absorption in the simulated war-game that he had forgotten for the moment that it was only practice. If it hadn't been for that commanding voice, he now realized, he might have given way to his blood lust and have plunged his long knife into the other's vitals.

"What Company are you attached to, private?" the Captain who stood near him, asked.

"The X— Company, Rangers, Lieut. Boyd in command," he replied.

"Men," the Captain said warmly, "you've seen as fine a demonstration of the Wrist-Breach-and-Knee-Attack as you may witness at any time."

"Private," he continued, "you may go on and join your company. Give me your name and I'll report the capture of my man to your commander. I'm sure he'll be proud of you. You must come over to our company and give us another demonstration of that action you carried out."

Zsimanski slogged back along the road he knew his company to have gone and when he caught up with it, the maneuver was over.

His story, when he told it to his comrades, sounded flukey, but the promotion he got to two stripes and the increase in pay were substantial proof of his claims.

Zsimanski was learning and learning fast.

REAR WAIST BREACH

"Attention, men," boomed Lieut. Boyd. "I know you're as proud of Corporal Zsimanski as I am, but that glorious victory, you know, hasn't downed a single Jap or Hun. And," he continued in his dry lower register, "maybe it's a secret to you, but that's what we're really here for."

"Well," a voice whispered, "we ain't gonnna talk 'em to death neither."

"The guard house for you, Private Simpkins, not for insubordination — although it might well be — but for dreaming on your feet and talking in your sleep," snapped the Lieutenant.

Simpkins stepped out of the ranks and slouched towards the barracks, his lips moving in what the company took to be no prayer.

"Now, with that interruption over, let's proceed," commanded the Lieutenant.

"What we're going to learn today," he went on, "is the Rear-Waist-Breach.

"Stone, Harlow, step forward. Face each other.

"Now, Stone, you step behind Harlow. Put your arms around his waist with your biceps well up under his armpits. Hug him tight. You, Stone, grasp your left wrist with the fingers of your right hand and squeeze."

"Sure, dearie," whispered Harlow, "kiss the lobe of my pink-shelled ear, while you're at it."

"Now, Harlow," asked the Lieutenant, "what would you do to get out of that hold?"

"Tickle him in the ribs," grinned Harlow.

"This is serious," the Lieut. scowled.

"Well, then I'd huff and I'd puff...."

"Latrine humor," the Lieut. commented bitterly. "You, Harlow, close that gap only your mother thinks is a mouth and pay attention.

"Just bend forward at the waist.

"Clasp both hands together, lacing your fingers. Then hunch either your right or your left shoulder, and as Stone stands right behind you, lift one of your elbows up and strike him in the jaw."

"It's a pleasure," Harlow grinned.

"Ouch," Stone howled. "He broke my jaw."

"Oh, come on Stone, as long as you can still talk he can't have broken your jaw. Besides, it's only practice. Notice men, Stone had to let go. Harlow has breached the waist hold from the rear."

"Pardon me, dearie," Harlow said with mock contrition to Stone, "Commander's orders. Not that I ain't had any fun doing it for you."

This is a diagram of the action:

CIRCUS MULE TRICK

"Feeling pretty good, aren't you?" asked Lieut. Boyd of Private Harlow. You're a man after my own heart. But I daresay, Stone might well be after yours. You can dish it out. Can you take it?"

"Yes, sir, Lieutenant," said Harlow proudly. "I'll take it—but I won't like it."

"Harlow," continued the Lieutenant, "you get behind Stone, this time. Put your arms around Stone's waist, as you saw him do you. Clasp your right hand fingers around your left wrist and squeeze as hard as you can."

"I know," said Stone eagerly, "I clasp my two hands together and hump my shoulders, and then bring up shoulder right into his jaw. Please, Lieutenant, let me do it. Will you. I'll score a knockout as sure as shootin'."

"No, no, not this time."

"Aw, Lieutenant, it ain't fair," said Stone resentfully.

"Attention!" Stone subsided with a frown.

"Now, Stone, spread your feet apart widely.

"Bend forward at the waist.

"Now grab Harlow's ankle. Either one of them. But with both hands. Got it?"

"Oh boy, have I!" Stone exulted.

"All right, now sit down. That's right. Right down on Harlow. Throw yourself backwards. He's got a thick head. It won't knock him out."

"So he's down, Lieut. What do I do next?"

"You haven't let go your grip on his ankle, have you?"

"No."

"Then let go one of your hands. I suggest your releasing your right hand from his ankle.

"Then grasp his foot at the toes. Got that?"

"Sure, Lieut. Ain't I havin' fun!"

"Now, bend his leg backwards towards his hip. And TWIST his toe with your right hand while you twist his ankle with your left.

"If you do it hard enough—and don't you dare—you can either break his toes or snap his ankle."

"You mean, I gotta let up short of breakin' his toe or ankle," queried Stone anxiously.

"I mean just that."

"Can't I give him just one break? Just one little break."

"That's enough," the Lieutenant shouted. "Get up."

"Now have you got that, boys? Then try that Circus Mule Trick again, only this time let Harlow be in front of you, Stone. And boys," he turned to the rest of the company, "pair off, each two of you and try the Circus Mule Trick. Hop to it!"

Would you like a picture of the trick? Here it is:

Again opponent grabs you from rear under your arms.

Spread your feet so they are to the right and left of his.

Bend forward, your feet spread widely apart and grab his right or left leg by ankle (with your both wrists).

Then sit down backwards on top of him. Then change your position by releasing one hand (right) from his ankle and grasping his toes. Bend his leg backwards against his hip and twist toe and ankle.

Both will snap and since you are sitting on top of him, he'll be helpless.

MODIFIED FLYING-MARE

"Who'll volunteer for the next trick?" asked Lieut. Boyd of his company. "Of course I can't promise any of you the D. S. C. for stepping forward. But one of you might get hurt. Is there a man in the house?"

"Sure" said Pee-wee Roush, "I'm your man, Lieutenant, what there is of me."

"Fine, fine," said the Lieut., "size doesn't make the man. The Japs are small but they're terrible fighters. And besides Judo is the great equalizer. You mustn't forget that it's a science. It's using your opponent's strength against him. Is there another man almost as good as Roush?"

"I'm not letting any runt consider him better than me," snarled Peters, stepping out of the ranks. "I'll take him on."

"All right, Peters," said Lieut. Boyd, "Stand in back of Roush and grasp him around the waist."

"Around the waist?" asked Peters. "I'll have to get down on my knees to take this grasshopper around the waist."

"Your girl ain't any bigger," smirked Roush, "and I seen you do a pretty good job of finding her waist."

"Shut your lip, you runt."

"All right, all right. Stow the gab boys," commanded the Lieutenant. "Ready?"

Peters finally found Pee-wee's waist and hugged him around it with his arms well under the other's arm-pits, squeezing until he felt the slighter man's ribs crack.

"This is my special Sunday night hold in the park," he whispered.

"She ain't gonna live long enough to neck," gasped Pee-wee, "if that's the way you do it. Let up, you bum."

"Now, Roush," went on the Lieutenant, "interlock your fingers in front of you. Press your elbows outward. Come on, push them outward with all your might. Feel his hold weakening?"

"Now push your left foot backward between Peter's legs. But press firmly down on your right foot to give you good balance. Got it?

"Now unclasp your hands. Reach over with your left hand and grasp his right sleeve or his wrist; and grasp his left wrist or sleeve with your right hand.

"Tighten your grips. With real force.

"Then bend your right leg slightly at the knee. Just enough to give you a sort of pedestal to rest on.

"Now bend your body forward at the waist. Twist your body a little to the right, so you'll have a sort of lever of your right hip.

"Now strain yourself forward and HEAVE!

"That's it. Throw him over your left shoulder. LET GO OF YOUR HOLD ON HIS SLEEVES."

Peters flew through the air with the greatest of ease. He landed heavily on the ground.

And little Pee-wee brushed his hands gleefully.

"Lieutenant, that was a pip," he gloated. "It's worth a month's pay. I always wanted to brush that guy off."

"Well, Peters," asked the Lieutenant, "will you admit that in Judo a little man can be as good as the best big man?"

"Yeah," said Peters bewildered. "But supposing I was the guy in front, what would happen to a little guy like Pee-wee. You'd find nothing but a grease spot."

"Try it," said the Lieutenant, while Pee-wee looked up shocked.

And Peters did.

This is how it appeared when someone's candid camera caught the shot.

ARM PINION

Boat Co. X, Amphibian Regiment, were lined up under their new Commander, Captain Enos Barker. The service was new, the men a polygot collection of misfits, "un-fits" and "inepts" from other regiments and their commander a famous disciplinarian who had undertaken to whip these square pegs into round holes—and he was doing it.

The men had been drilling in broiling sun, in swamp and morass, over land and sea, until every muscle shrieked and every flank was lean and face was gaunt. Yet these caterwaulers from many services were being welded into a dangerous weapon for the defense of Democracy. They had no time to carp or crawl.

Captain Barker believed in Judo. In happier times and long before the sneak-punch at Pearl Harbor he had been military attache at Tokyo and while there had been steeped in Jigoro Kano's Kodokwan Judo. He knew and had downed the Japs' best.

For the past month, since the Service had been established, he had been teaching his men Judo.

"Today," he said in his quietly commanding manner, "we will study the Arm-Pinion."

"Study, did he say?" mouthed Jonesy to his buddy Tolliver. He had been "broken" more than once from Sergeant to private in his former billets, and had a certain "freshness" in talk and behavior to uphold. He was a sterling soldier except for this penchant to criticize. "Study? It'll probably be moider with three dees."

"Quit your yapping," Tolliver told him, his eyes rigid, only his lips moving furtively. "You're in line for Staff Sergeant again. The Cap's got his eye on you."

"His eye's as cold as a banker's heart," returned the irrepressible Jonesy. But he clamped his mouth shut almost at once.

"We'll want two men to demonstrate this hold," went on Captain Barker imperturbably, although he couldn't help but overhear the illict conversation. "You, Jones, and the next man to you, Tolliver, isn't it?"

"Yes, sir!" They both stepped out and saluted.

"Now, men, face each other." The boys did.

"Jones, you bring your left hand up, ball your fist and throw your left towards Tolliver.

"Hold it, I didn't say hit him with it.

"Well Tolliver, what would you do to ward off that left of Jones'?"

"Why, I'd bring up my right and hold it in front of my face, sir."

"Well, that would be all right ordinarily, but Judo has a better solution. You must not only be able to ward off a blow, but must be prepared, as any warrior should, to attack as well as defend. We are training to become the most offensive fighters in the world and Judo can help us.

"Now, as Jones throws his left at you....come on, try it again, Jones....you, Tolliver bring your right hand up and inside of his left forearm and make a wide outward sweep with your right forearm, pushing Jones' left aside.

"But, if you stop there, Jones may still bring his right over and hit you with it.

"Therefore," he paused, "grasp his right wrist with the fingers of your left hand before he has time to bring it up to attack. Grasp it so that your thumb digs into the inside of his wrist while your fingers grip the outer surface of his wrist rigidly and with all the force you can command.

"Thus far," he continued, "you have only defended yourself. His left arm is still free.

"You're in front of him. Keep holding his right wrist.

Step a pace or two to your left, pivot on your right heel and still holding on to his wrist, step behind Jones. Pull his right wrist and arm with you and press it against his back. Bend his elbow and pull it up his back.

"And then bring your right hand across his back and grab the point just above his elbow, pressing your right thumb deeply into the flesh at that point.

"See, you've got him pinioned. But he may still struggle. You therefore bend your left elbow inward so that the point of the elbow digs deep into his left shoulder blade.

"You can notice that as you exert more and more pressure, he is compelled to bend forward at the waist.

"If this were not practice, one of two things would happen, wouldn't it? Can you tell me what, Tolliver?"

"Yes, Captain, Sir," Tolliver replied with satisfaction. "Jones would have to fall forward from the pressure and pain in his back, in order to relieve the strain, or else I would pull his arm and with both hands on wrist and elbow I would dislocate the shoulder or crack the elbow bone."

"That's exactly right," said Captain Barker. "If it weren't for the fact that we need every man to fight our common enemy, I'd say, go to it, Tolliver. Sometimes a broken elbow or dislocated shoulder silences a sharp and ready tongue."

The words were hardly cryptic and thoroughly understood by both Jones and his fellow soldiers. They laughed with glee, but Jones only grinned a sickly grin. He had learned not to underestimate his commander.

If we were to draw a picture of what took place it would look something like this:

KNIFE COUNTER

"Say, Corp. Swanson," said Pvt. Tobin, "I hear by the Latrine Daily News that Captain Barker was on Bataan. Is that some more bull?"

"As a rule," answered the corporal, "anything you hear from that source might as well appear on Scot-Tissue, but in this instance it's absolutely correct. And what's more, he was wounded perhaps a dozen times."

"Gee," the other answered with awe, "you'd think a guy like that would rest on his laurels and retire on a pension."

"Oh, yeah?" replied Swanson scornfully, "he told me that if he had a wooden leg and a glass eye he'd still try to get back to Bataan eventually and pay back the scummy Japs for the treatment they dealt out to the heroic Filipinos. He had been a Colonel in the Constabulary at one time or another and he's got a warm spot in his heart for our little brown brothers."

"Yeah," said Tobin thoughtfully, "that kind of a guy'll die with his boots on, all right."

"Yes, and when they play taps over him, they'll probably find those boots resting their heels on the necks of a couple of dirty Nipponese barbarians."

"You know, Corp," went on Tobin, chewing his Spearmint, "that Knife-Counter trick of the Cap's is something special, but in spite of the many times I've seen it and tried it, I still haven't got it quite down to the science the Cap told us we must get it."

"Why, Tob, I didn't think it was very complicated."

"Would you mind showing me that set-up again, Corp," asked Tobin. "I know you seemed to get it at once the other day, but I'm slightly fuzzy about it yet."

"Well, now, let's face each other as we did in practice. You, Tob, get a stick, a short one, about the size of a kitchen knife. That's it, that little branch there.

"I'll stand to the left here and you stand to the left facing me."

A crowd of boys had gathered around them. It was after four-thirty and anything was good for a laugh.

"Homework, fellers," said the company clown, Murphy.

"Shame on you, Tobin," another jibed, "A Hibernian using a knife. What about a Shillela?"

The corporal and Tobin ignored the crowd and the badinage. "The hoi-polloi snickereth," commented the corporal, casually as if the interruption came from the bleachers in a ball park.

Tobin made a lunge for the corporal with his improvised knife. Swanson stepped one pace to his own left, then moved forward almost imperceptibly and seized the back of Tobin's wrist with the fingers of his right hand, holding it tightly.

"Watch this closely," he said to Tobin.

He pushed the knife-clutching hand forward and away from the position of his body, raising the hand as high as he could.

Then he threw himself sideways, so that his body rested on his right palm on the ground. His right leg he pushed way behind him and rested firmly on the ball of his right foot.

"From here on the action must be fast, so pay close attention," he cautioned.

He lifted his left leg up extended rigidly in front of him and drew it across the front of Tobin's thighs, just above the knees.

Then balancing himself on his right palm on the ground, he brought up his right leg in back of the inside of the knee joints of Tobin, and then twined the instep of his right foot around the instep of his left foot, making a clamp or vise around the thighs of Tobin.

"This you see," he told Tobin, "is like a lobster-crawl, and my legs act as a pincer around your thighs."

"Two to one on the cockroach," shouted Murphy the Kibitzer.

"He looks like a pretzel," said another. "It'll take a derrick to unscramble them when it's over."

"Don't pay any attention to the gallery," panted Swanson. "Just look from here on."

He pressed backward on Tobin's knife-hand and exerted a mighty heave on his own locked legs and threw Tobin backward onto the ground. All this while he had kept firm hold on Tobin's knife arm.

The fall jarred Tobin a bit and he was slightly dizzy.

Swanson pulled out his left leg from under the other's thigh, shifted his position and got on top and astride of the fallen soldier. His left hand still held the right and knife-hand wrist of Tobin.

"To get the knife out of harm's way," he went on in a quieter tone, "I must do something now or all my work will be for nothing."

He thereupon brought over his right hand releasing his left hand from the wrist of Tobin, brought the left hand under the other's right arm and clasped his own right wrist, which had just seized the knife-hand of Tobin.

With the weight of his pushing right hand against the wrist of Tobin and his own left hand helping to force pressure on the knife-hand of Tobin, he held Tobin powerless.

"Now, if we were really in a mortal fight," said Swanson, "I would press so hard that I would either break your arm or at least dislocate your shoulder."

"As it is, do you feel the pressure?" he asked.

"Do I?" gasped Tobin. "I'll have to give up and drop the knife unless you relieve the pressure."

"That's just what anyone would do, except a Jap. He'd never give up. So, he continued calmly, "I'd just break his wrist or dislocate his arm. And for good measure," he went on ominously, "when his arm is broken, I'd let go his arm and give him my fist between the eyes."

"Hey, that wouldn't be cricket," said one of the kidders who were watching.

"No," returned Swanson, "I don't know if the Asian New Order ever heard of the game. Knife-in-the-back is a game nearer to their hearts."

The various movements the corporal and the private went through may be analyzed in pictures as follows:

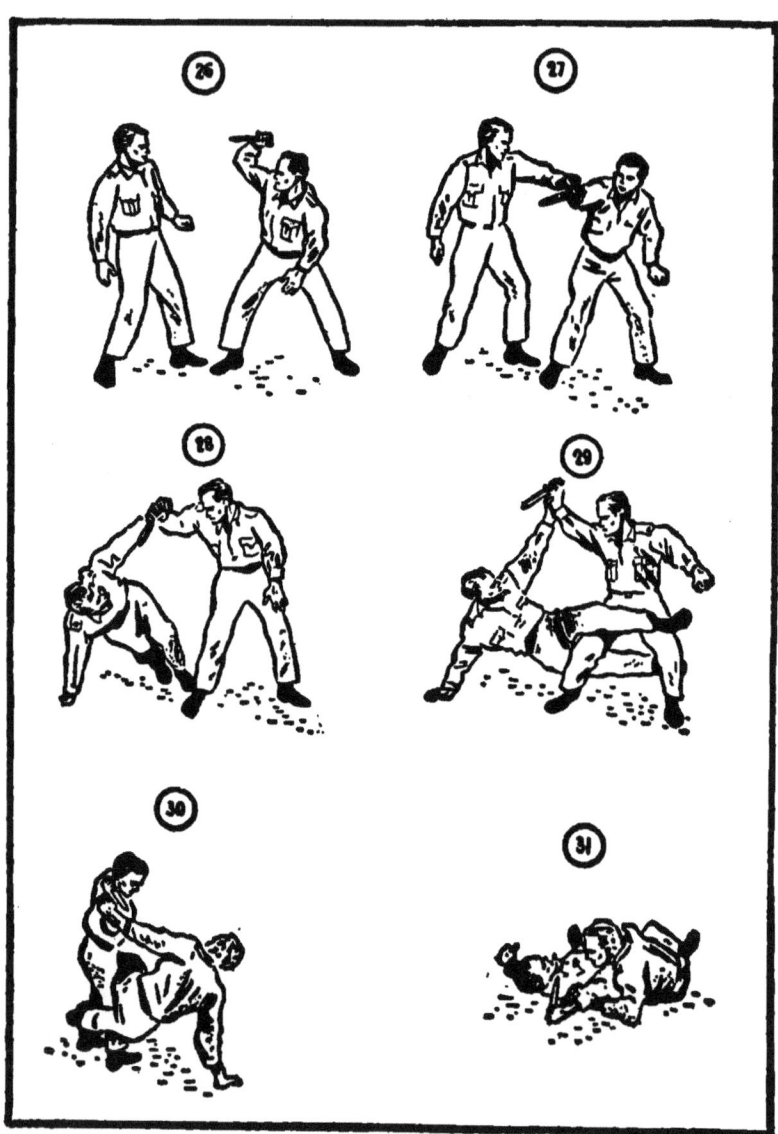

STRANGLE HOLD

"Today," said Captain Barker in his inimitable Vermont dry twang, "we have a pleasant lesson. We're going to choke a man."

The laugh, if he expected any, was dutifully forthcoming, though all of the men knew one of them would be picked to be the victim and it would hardly be pleasant.

"Now, it may seem to you, men, that it is a simple matter to choke a man. And it would be if your opponent were a lay figure and would just offer his neck for slaughter. Our friend, the enemy, however, might have a very healthy objection and besides, he too might know Judo. Don't forget the Japs have all been taught that science almost from infancy."

"Then how can we compete?" asked one of the men reasonably.

"That's a legitimate question, and I welcome it," replied Captain Barker. "Dont be afraid to speak up, men. We may learn from logical criticism.

"In the first place," he continued, "it is my contention that our free way of life, our free schools and athletic sports have given us free minds that will grasp anything quicker. A regimented mind may do a thing methodically, may even do it thoroughly, but it is taught to await a command. I maintain that in a pinch, where a question of free choice confronts us, the habit of mind brought about by freedom to think along original lines will cause you to be more resourceful, will make you grasp opportunities better."

"But Judo follows certain rules," returned the critic unabashed, "and our enemies know those rules better than we do. You said so yourself."

"That's right. They do. And on the mat in a gymnasium they might have every advantage. But, men, battles are not fought by rules of conduct, the battlefields are not always chosen by your opponent. Besides you are all grown-ups; you should be able to grasp ideas more quickly and with free, investigative faculties, profit better than obedient slaves of the State such as are the Japs or the Huns."

"Let's see if what I say isn't a fact. You, Parker, who justly questioned your own ability to learn quickly. I'll use you in this experiment. You'll do the choking, and you'll do it with a minimum of instruction. Before you do anything I'm going to ask you what you would do. We'll see if it works."

"Newton, step forward.

"Stand with your back facing Parker.

"Parker, since you are in back of Newton, how would you go about choking him?"

"Well, sir, I could put my hands around his neck. But," thoughtfully, "he's got quite a big neck. He might struggle and break my hold as soon as he feels my hands around his neck."

"That's right. What other way could you possibly get his neck in such a hold that you would shut off his windpipe? It would naturally have to be some part of your body that could encircle his neck completely."

"I know, I know," said Parker quickly, "I could put my arm around his neck and draw my forearm across his neck in front, pressing my forearm against his throat. That would hold him, all right."

"That's correct. Do it, but don't press too tight as yet. Use your right arm."

"Now, that you have the hold, how could you keep it? He could still struggle out of it, couldn't he? You have to clamp that hold in some way."

"I got it," Parker replied. "I must hold my right arm with my left and so encircle him completely."

"Yes. But pressure must be exerted if you are to choke off any outcry. Don't you think you can do it in such a way as to give you the greatest leverage?"

"Sure," said Parker. "I could grab my right hand with my left and pull on it."

"That's just it. Only you have to hold your right hand in such a way as to leave you free to make any other move you might want. Suppose you hold your right hand fingers together and form a sort of hook and hook your left hand fingers the same way, hooking them into the right hand fingers. Like this."

"I notice you stand directly in back of Newton with your feet together. What will you do, keep him up-right all the time? If so, you will be as much a prisoner of your own hold as he."

"I understand, Captain. I've got to throw him down. I'll put one foot back, my left foot, that will give me leverage, and step back a bit from him, while I still hold onto his neck. And I could put my right leg, bent at the knee, under the inside of the knee joint of one of his legs. That will bend him back. See, now he rests his head on my right shoulder."

"That's precisely what I meant," said the Captain with satisfaction. "But you still haven't got him down."

"Well," mused Parker, "I could get him down on one knee."

"That's it. That's it," shouted the Captain.

"Now all you have to do is to bend him backward as far as he'll go. Bring his neck down across your knee, and if he struggles, break his neck across your knee. Got it?"

"Hey, Cap," gulped Newton feebly, "I-I-I'm chokin'. Let up. Will you."

"Yes, you can let him go, now," said Captain Barker. "There's no use breaking a neck we'll need to help us get back Bataan." He said it grimly. His eyes were slits of hate. And then he smiled. "Newton might try it on his lady-friend. It might be called necking, also."

STRADDLE-CHOKE

"It goes without saying," said Captain Barker, "that if you are at all squeamish about the damage you may do to an enemy you don't belong in the Army.

"I wouldn't worry about that turn-your-other-cheek philosophy," he went on, "in the midst of battle, for," he smiled knowingly, "you'd lose that quickly if you saw the ferocity in the slant eyes of the foe and you knew it was his life or yours. Self-preservation is stronger than sentiment. But lack of hate makes you weaker in determination. If you have learned to measure the virulence of your opposition, you are forewarned and thus forearmed.

"I want you to become rough, to think tough. Even if you think of it as a game, play to kill. After all that's what we are training for—to kill as many of our enemies as we can. They, too, are training along similar lines. We must—to paraphrase a public speaker of note—get there fustest with the mostest—and the worstest."

"This, gentlemen," he told the company, "is by way of introduction to our lesson. We are going to learn the Straddle-Choke."

He chose two of the Privates, and asked all the others to pair off and take positions exactly as the two he had chosen would be directed to take.

"Let's assume, men," he said, "that we are attacking. We have landed our Amphibian Boat and we have disembarked.

"It's night. Pitch dark. You can barely see your hand in front of your nose. You encounter opposition. It's each man for himself.

"Somehow, you Miller," he addressed one of the two Privates that stood before the assembled company, "have lost your gun; your side arm is in your holster. You stumble upon Moran, there, whom you are to suppose is one of the enemy. You haven't time to pull your pistol out. He is about to attack you.

"I don't care how you do it. Punch him, or trip him, or hug him until you have him on the ground. There's no such thing as fair play in this sort of combat. Neither of you is thinking of anything but killing the other.

"Moran, get on the ground. Assume that you have been thrown down on your back."

Moran did as he was told and stretched out.

"Now, Miller, jump astride him. Whoa! I was only supposing. I didn't say jump on him with your shoes. Get astraddle of him, as though you were riding a horse. That's it. Kneel astride of him.

Grasp his coat lapel with your left hand. Then reach across underneath your left hand, and with your right hand grasp his right coat lapel.

What's the object of that, you will ask? Why don't you grab his right coat lapel with your left hand and his left coat lapel with your right hand? Well, you wouldn't be able to exert any pressure against his throat.

"You see, Miller," he continued "when you have crossed your arms in the fashion I have just shown you, you can form a sort of cross-pull, which, with intense pressure and pull, can help to garrot or choke him.

"Also, as you note, since you are kneeling, all you need do, is bend your left elbow, and the point of it will come in contact with his Adam's Apple. You should press the point of your elbow hard.

"But in addition to that, still astride him, pulling and pressing on his coat lapels in this cross-cut manner, you should sort of fall, or roll over on your left shoulder, continuing the pressure and pull of your hands against his lapels, but your right hand at his right coat lapel should serve two purposes. It should keep his coat tight around his neck and the knuckles of your right hand should grind into his throat with force and great determination."

"Of course," he said as he noticed Moran's slightly livid appearance and faint gurgle, "now you may let up. I don't intend to have you kill Moran. But remember, when you have a Jap or a Heinie under you and you are attempting to choke him in the manner described, don't let up until you feel that he is unconscious or dead. It may sound grisly, but the best enemy is a dead one."

"I'm going to make a diagram for you on the Barrack's Blackboard so you can study it at your leisure."

This was the picture he drew.

BENT-ARM STRADDLE CHOKE

"You know, Captain," said Lieut. Purdy warmly, as he sat to the right of the commanding officer in the Officers' Mess," the morale of the men is something wondrous to behold. I honestly believe that this Judo you have introduced in their training is just the catalyst that was needed to weld as diverse a set of humans into one homogenous group as I've ever seen."

"It's nice of you to say so, Lieutenant," smiled Captain Barker. "I felt it myself but I'd never be able to say it so beautifully. By the way, Lieutenant, don't think me impertinent, but what were you in civil life?"

"Just a humble professor of psychology, Captain," the other replied with a deprecatory laugh.

"I thought as much. Maybe you haven't noticed it, Lieutenant, but it was a source of wonder and no little dismay to me at first when I discovered that the boys in our command were almost a complete cross-section of our country, one or more from every nook and cranny of our large and small cities, from farm and mill and factory, and some from our best Halls of Learning. I must say I have imbibed a greater faith in democracy from just being with these boys."

"Yes," said Purdy, "it's a liberal education to all of us. Their spirit is wonderful. I must say that in the past I never gave much credit for intelligence to the so-called common man. You see, from my ivory tower, I never really knew my fellow man. I saw only the select few who could afford to be subjected to four years of education. I must confess I was no little bit pedantic in my approach to my subject."

"Well," rejoined the Captain, "you certainly have an invaluable opportunity of doing clinical research right here in our Company. And, Lieutenant," with the slightest bit of friendly malice, "I hope you don't dissect any of them too thoroughly. Most people hate to be guinea pigs."

"Oh, no," rather hastily, "don't misunderstand me, Captain. I've shed my pedagogue's penchant for the duration. I think the boys have accepted me for just another Looey."

"That's fine, but really fine," enthused the Captain. "And Lieut. Purdy, I want you to take over the next lesson in Judo. So, if you'll please be good enough to come to our improvised gym, I want to show you the hold I call the Bent-Arm Straddle Choke. I've had a call from G. H. Q. and expect to be away for a few days. You'll have to take over."

The two officers left the Mess Hall and wended their way to the gym.

"Lieutenant," the Captain said, "let's shed this formality for the moment. Your first name, I understand, is Clinton. I'll call you Clint, if you'll call me Jim. I could hardly choke a man and continue to call him Lieutenant Clinton Purdy, can I?".

"Why, of course, Jim. Thanks."

"Now, Clint, I may be rough, but I can't demonstrate this hold unless I am, and it may hurt a bit. I'll try not to be too brutal."

"Shoot, Jim. And devil take the hindmost. What's good enough for the men is good enough for me."

"Now, you'll be the underdog, Clint. So please get down on the mat on your back."

"Done."

"All right. Now I straddle you. With my knees. That is, I get astride of you and rest on my knees to each side of your body.

"I grasp your left lapel, as close to your neck as possible with my left hand.

"Then I snake my right arm around and under your head and directly in back of your neck; then catch and hold my own left arm either at the wrist or by the sleeve.

"You'll notice that when I bend forward, as I'm doing now, my left elbow is pressing directly at your throat.

"You're practically helpless already, aren't you?"

Only a nod showed Purdy's assent.

"Of course, Clint, this isn't a very good demonstration, because if I really wanted to hurt you or throw you into unconsciousness, all I have to do is to increase the pressure against your windpipe by pushing with my left forearm and at the same time pull my left arm tighter around your throat by pulling with my right arm, and lean to the left.

"Should I desire to choke you to death, it would be simple, if I fell over onto my own left shoulder. The force of my fall and the pressure on your throat would shut off your wind altogether."

He released his hold and got off the mat.

"Do you think you have it, Clint?"

"Has he got it?" chorused an impromptu audience. "Let's see you do it again, Cap."

"Yeah, that was a pip, only it didn't go far enough," said another.

The two officers took the kidding good-naturedly, as it was indeed meant.

"You'll see it again, boys," Captain Barker told them. "Lieutenant Purdy is going to give you all an opportunity of using the Bent-Arm-Straddle Choke tomorrow."

Amid a chorus of groans, the crowd dispersed.

To illustrate, this is the way the Bent-Arm-Straddle Choke was done by the boys after Lieutenant Purdy conducted the formation the next day.

STRANGLE BREACH

"You will note," said Capt. Barker, "that in practically all our lessons we have discussed and demonstrated offensive tactics; how to attack and dispose of an enemy who is himself attacking."

"Yes," muttered Pvt. Hymie Kaplan, "as if them Japs don't know their own Judo. Just waiting for us to grab 'em and put 'em down."

As if he had heard the "beef," Capt. Barker went on, "It's hardly to be expected that our enemies will wait patiently for us to pick our spots, let us get the best holds we know and then gracefully fold up to accommodate us. Just remember, fellows, that the Jap is an aggressive, cruel, mean and treacherous fighter. If there ever was a time when Judo carried with it a spirit of courtliness and politeness—fairplay to you—the Jap leaders, with their contempt for all other races, have long since eradicated all trace of it. The Jap soldier is now an efficient murder weapon."

"Oh, yeah," shouted Pugliesi involuntarily, forgetting his soldierly decorum, his hot blood boiling dangerously, "we'll moider dem Japs. Any Yank's as good as ten Japs."

"That's a popular fallacy," smiled Captain Barker, not at all disturbed by this outburst. "Never underestimate your enemy."

"Step forward, young fellow," he said quietly. "What's your name?" "Private Rocco Pugliesi, Sir," said the soldier, a bit taken aback. 'I didn't mean nothin', Sir. I was just sore, I guess."

"Sore, he says," whispered Kaplan, "that guy's always boiling like a hot borscht."

"Sure," agreed Mike O'Reilly next to him, "that Spaghettibender is hotter'n a red pepper. But I'll put him up against any Jap or Heinie anywhere."

"Now, Pvt. Pugliesi," said Capt. Barker, "let's forget the odds you chose. Ten to one may or may not be the exact number you'll encounter when you get to the front, but for the sake of argument we'll assume that you now have to deal with only one, lone, single Jap."

"You, there," he pointed to Private Hymie Kaplan, "you don't look much like a Jap, but let's pretend you are. Suppose you stand there facing Pugliesi."

"Face him," muttered Hymie, "I can hardly look at him."

"Shut up, you ape," grated Rocco good-naturedly, "if it wasn't for the Cap. here, I wouldn't need no Judo to mobilize you."

"You and the Swiss Navy," snickered Hymie.

"Come, come boys," admonished the Captain, "save your persiflage for the next Tea Social. You're not a comedy vaudeville team, you know.

"Now, Kaplan, you stand right in front of Pugliesi. You're goin to choke him."

"It's a pleasure," chortled Kaplan.

"Pugliesi, you back up against this wall here. You see Kaplan, the Jap, approaching and you don't want anybody behind you.

"Kaplan, extend your hands stiffly in front of you. Put your arms around his neck. Grasp it firmly, as if you actually were going to dig your thumbs into his windpipe. Now I said 'as if,' remember.

"You, Pugliesi, you haven't time to consider what to do to Kaplan. You can't plan an attack when his hands are on your throat. You just simply have to break that hold. What would be the best thing to do?"

"Well," he continued, "there are a number of ways that hold could be broken. We'll take up one at a time.

"Pugliesi, bring up your arms, shoulder height. Now, grab his arms on the outside of his elbows.

"Press your thumbs into the hollow of his arms, just above the elbow joints. But press with great force. As if your life depended upon it. As indeed it would.

"Now crook your own elbows and pull outward on Kaplan's arms. Now. Suddenly. With muscle-grease.

"That's it. Notice how his arms give way? You've broken the hold. Now, step away to either your left or right.

"That, gentlemen," said Captain Barker, "might be said to be the strangle-breach by 'pull'.

"Stand where you are, boys. We'll try another. We'll now break the same hold by 'push'."

STRANGLE-BREACH BY "PUSH"

"Kaplan," grinned Captain Barker, " you've had your fun. Now, you take Pugliesi's place. He's going to choke you.

"Oh boy, oh boy," cried Rocco, "there's gonna be a choked herring around here."

"Come on, Pug, put your hands in front of you. Extend your arms stiffly. Kaplan, you take your place against the wall.

"Get your fingers curled around Kap's neck. Squeeze with some force, but don't actually strangle him. That's it."

"Let me finish it," begged Pugliesi.

Kaplan stuck out his tongue as though he were really being asphyxiated, although it looked suspiciously like a childish gesture of defiance.

"Kaplan, you've got to break that hold around your neck. But you're not going to do it by pulling his arms as Pug did to you.

"Just bend your arms at the elbows, making a right-angle upwards. That's right. Now insert your arms bent upwards in this fashion between Pug's arms around your neck. Then interlace your fingers, making a sort of tent of your arms.

"Now, quickly and with all the speed and force you can command, plunge your arms and elbows outward and against Pug's arms.

"That's it. You're pushing them apart. Yes, that's the simple way to break an ordinary choke-hold around your neck by "push".

"Of course," said Capt. Barker, "there are other ways of breaking a choke-hold. One is the

BODY BLOW or SOLAR PLEXUS PUNCH

"While your opponent has his arms extended in front of you and is attempting to choke you by hugging your neck

with his hands, you can ball the fist of your right hand, extending the knuckle of your second finger, bent at the joint so as to form a sort of hob-nail extending from your fist. Then rap suddenly and with great force against the muscles of your opponent's stomach, right in the pit of it, above the navel. That, as you undoubtedly know, is what is called the 'Solar Plexus',

"It will give him sufficient pain to have him drop his hands from your neck to defend his stomach."

"Or," the Captain went on, "you could use the

DOUBLE-KNUCKLE SCREW

"This sounds more complicated than it is.

"It merely means—and the term is used for convenience in talking about it only—that when your opponent is endeavoring to choke you by holding you around the throat, and you still have all your faculties, you ball both your fists, leaving the bent knuckles of your third fingers of each hand, out in the knob-like manner I have already indicated.

"Then you bring those knuckles in a sharp tattoo rap against your opponent's stomach at the lower ends of his ribs on his right and left side.

"The pain there will be so sharp that he will have to drop his hands.

"There's still another way to break the choke-hold," continued the Captain. "We may call it, if you wish, the

UPWARD BATTERING-RAM

"When your foe's arms are around your neck as we have already noted, your arms and hands are free. If, of course, the choking has gotten you to the point where you are unable to coordinate your mind and muscle, there's little you can do. But if you are still conscious and can still control your limbs, the choke-hold is easily broken.

"Join your hands below your waist, by lacing your fingers together, but your arms must be in front of you.

"Then, with extraordinary speed and force, using your joined hands like a battering ram, plunge them upward, bending your elbows vertically, and smack your joined hands against either his right or left elbow joint.

"The force of your blow is sure to break his hold around your neck. And from then on, you will have to consider means of destroying him."

STRANGLE BREACH FOLLOW-UP

"You will wonder, I suppose," lectured Captain Barker, "why we have spent so much time on the Strangle-Hold and its defense."

"Seems them Japs don't do nothing but go around choking guys," piped up Mugs O'Toole. "Why don't the doity scuts fight like men? A sock on the beezer oughta make 'em behave."

"That's right, O'Toole," said Capt. Barker surprisingly. "I was coming to that. Only when some one has his arms up in front of you and his hands are choking your neck, you havent much time, room or leverage for a good, healthy swing on his beezer.

"Let's see how we can accomplish the same thing, only much more scientifically and quickly.

"O'Toole, you're the socker. Let Simmons, here, stand in front of you and grasp you around the neck with both his hands.

"Well, O'Toole, now that Simmons is choking you, let's see how you would sock him on the beezer."

O'Toole was a bit put out. Simmons seemed to take his work seriously and was putting on the pressure, so that the little fighter from Tenth Avenue felt his eyes begin to bulge. His arms were paralyzed to some extent.

"Now, you see, O'Toole," went on the Captain inexorably, "you can't very well swing your arms. He's got you in a pretty bad way. Let up a bit, Simmons.

"Well, we know how to break that hold first. Don't we, O'Toole? Sure, we do. Just bring your arms up crooked at the elbow, interlace your fingers, and push your arms inside and between the extended arms of Simmons as he chokes you. Then push out your elbows smartly against his arms.

"See, he's had to let go.

"But you still want to injure him in return. You **want** to sock him on the beezer.

"Well, don't unclasp your interlaced hands.

"Just bring them up a little higher, and then with **your** hands still tented, bring them down on the bridge of **his** nose. Don't take me literally, O'Toole. I know you feel **bad** enough to annihilate Simmons, but he was only **obeying** instructions.

"I can assure you, without your actually carrying out the movement, that if you did bring your clasped hands down on his proboscis you would break his nose. The pain and the claret flowing from that snout would make him give up the battle.

"And still another way, to follow up the strangle-breach, after you have pushed his hands away from your throat, is to maneuver your body, so that you get behind him, or even if you are in front of him, keep your hands tented and clasped together, and bring the ram down on the back of your opponent's neck.

"The force of your clenched hands will fell him as if he were clouted with a singletree.

"And if you cannot get in position to use the battering ram on his nose, or in back of his neck, or even if you can, there is still another way to put him out of commission.

"After you have pushed his arms away from your neck and stopped his choke, you may bring up your bent right or left knee with considerable force under his testicles, in between his legs and in the crotch of his pants.

"That, my boys," he said sardonically, "has put many a good man down."

HAIR-PULL AND PUNISHMENT

Captain Barker looked at the determined faces of his new charges, the WAACS, and an inner warmth spread through his veins. These were no bored debu-tramps, or emancipated spinsters. They were all earnest, determined girls, eager to do their bit in the united War effort and grimly resolved to take all that was coming to them, whether of hardship or death.

There were one or two that were pretty enough to be, or to have been motion picture actresses while others looked as though hardships were not foreign to their background.

"Soldiers," he told them in ringing tones, "I won't insult you by addressing you as ladies. In the present state of world barbarism rampant that's an outworn title. It smacks of the drawing room—and you left it behind you for the duration. You'll have to be tough—as tough as any other soldier, for you'll see service with our men. You may not shoot a gun or throw a grenade or fly a bomber, but, his voice took on an ominous tone, "you may suffer attack just as all other soldiers. You must learn to take care of yourselves. You must be prepared to defend yourselves. Our enemies are no respecters of womanhood. You are in mortal peril unless you can use your knowledge and whatever strength you possess to attack as well as defend yourselves, personally.

"Now," he smiled, "with that off my chest, we can proceed with one of the lessons in defense and offense.

"One of the commonest assaults you may meet, perhaps because you are women, is the Hair-Pull hold. Now, don't smile. It may sound like something out of your distant past. And you may think that, as you probably have already demonstrated in your careers, two can play at the same game. But this isn't a game. If a Jap grabs you by the hair, and it will be only natural that he will think of that first, he means to kill. He knows no mercy or noblesse oblige. He's a barbarian who will strike and maim man, woman and child.

"Let's assume then that one of you has been attacked and that the brown beast has you by the hair. He's standing in front of you. You, soldier," he pointed to a slim, trim Goddess in uniform in the front row, "what's your name? Your last name. I can't keep saying 'you' when I address you."

"Jamieson, Sir," the WAAC told him in a clear voice.

"Step forward, Jamieson. The soldier next to you. What's your name?"

"Noble, Sir."

"All right, Noble, you face Jamieson. Jamieson, grab her by the hair in front. Get a good, firm grip.

"Now, Noble, don't obey that impulse. Don't pull away from that grip. If you do, she'll only hold harder and you may lose a tress or two of that beautiful auburn hair.

"Just lift your arm; and keep your head forward, pressing it against the hand that's holding your hair; that will minimize the pressure.

"Then grasp Jamieson's right wrist with your left hand.

"Advance your left foot forward, and step a pace to her right; no, don't twist your body. Keep facing her. That is correct.

"Insert your right arm under Jamieson's left (right) arm above the elbow, bending your forearm upward, grabbing at her right arm with your fingers pressing into her upper arm muscle.

"While you are doing that, press your left hand against her right wrist and press both arms forward, bending her arm backwards. That's right. Push your shoulder against her upper arm.

"What do you suppose will happen, if you use all the force you possess? Well, either you'll break her arm or the pain will make her give up her hold.

"Now, if you really want to break her arm, you can fall forward to the ground, still holding on to the wrist and arm you have secured and keep bending her arm and wrist backwards and outwards. She'll have to follow you to the ground, or her arm will snap into splinters."

The following is a diagram of what took place between Jamieson and Noble, soldiers extraordinary of the U. S. A.

Bend head forward and grasp right wrist with your left hand.

Insert your right arm under his left arm above elbow and grasp his bicep with your fingers.

With both your arms, one grasping his bicep and the other his wrist—bend his arm and wrist backward and outward. He must fall back and down or have his arm snap at worst.

Then drop to your knee.

PUNCH-THROW COUNTER

"WAACS," grinned the Captain, "I've been more than delighted with the way you have taken to Judo. When you get back to civilian life—and we hope that will be soon—after our enemies have been destroyed, you can laugh in the face of any man who tells you war is a man's game only. You can wipe the supercilious smirk off any "fresh-guy's" face by showing him that you, too, can stop a puncher."

"You mean," quavered one of the sturdy WAACS, "that the Japs or the Germans will actually try to punch us?"

"Listen," said the Captain seriously, "I thought you understood this was War, with a capital W? Do you think that if you stood in the path of a juggernaut it would politely side-step and pass you by so you could try to destroy it from the rear?

"No, soldier," he continued, "I don't think the Japs or the Germans or even the courtly Italians will try to punch you. I'm sure of it. They will, if they can, and if you are not ready to stop them. That's precisely what we are going to learn to do today.

"As long as you raised the question, Terry," he told her, "you might as well volunteer to be a victim of just such an attack."

Terry straightened her body and squared her cute little chin. "Yes, sir," she answered, "of course."

We'll use you, Sanford, that's your name, isn't it?"

"Now, Sanford, take a position facing Terry. And raise your hands in front of you, just as you must have seen boxers doing hundreds of times in the movies and out. That's right.

"Make a lunge with your left hand, Sanford. Of course you have balled your fist, haven't you. A boxer doesn't use a ladylike gesture such as a slap. He throws a fist. and it's usually his left. You'll find that to be a fact.

"All right, Terry, your first instinct will be to draw back to avoid the punch, won't it?"

"That's just what I was going to do," agreed Terry.

Well, don't do it. Don't be afraid of that punch. Step forward instead of backwards and grab her fist in both your hands.

"But continue going forward by extending your right foot forward.

"The twist her fisted hand inward toward her body toward her right, and move closer to her so that you may avoid her right fist which she surely would think of trowing towards you.

"Make it a strong twist. She'll never expect you to come in close instead of retreating. She'll never think you were going to grab her fist. The suddeness of your twist and the movement of your body inward will throw her to the ground. Am I right? That's it.

PUNCH-THROW COUNTER (continued)

"WAACS, I'm assuming that you are not children," Captain Barker, said, "and that you have some elementary notions of anatomy. There are certain portions of the human body that are more vulnerable than others. And the fact that you know the facts of life shouldn't deter you from using that knowledge to the best advantage against an enemy.

"Suppose, then, that a Jap was coming on to attack you, and when he got to a point where he was directly in front of you, he threw a punch toward you?

"We have learned that you could stop him by grabbing his fist and twisting it to throw him down to the ground.

"Today we will go further than that. We will learn that we can put him out of commission definitely and finally.

"I'd rather talk about this than demonstrate it, because I believe I can describe the action just as well. Then you'll all pair off and try it among yourselves.

"First we have the Jap coming at us. Then he's throwing a punch with his left hand.

"This time we won't grab his fist. We bend to the right at the waist. Clasp our hands tightly together, interlacing our fingers. This is to give us leverage and concentrate all our strength in the next action.

"When your body is bent over very low and almost parallel with the ground, you lift your left leg and with all the force you can muster you kick him in the crotch with an upward motion, so that the point of your shoe hits him right in the groin.

"You need have no fear that he will continue coming towards you. That is the most excrutiatingly dangerous place to strike a human that can be imagined.

"If your aim is good, and it must be, he'll fall to the ground writhing with pain and anguish."

This is the action as described:

CROTCH KICK COUNTER

"Don't think for one moment that because you are a woman, our enemies will try merely to scare you and cow you by mere words or by ferocious faces. The Jap has been taught to subdue an opponent, man or woman, catch-as-catch-can, and a barroom brawl will be a The Dansant compared to the tricks he will play to get an advantage. He'll kick, too, if he can.

"Now WAACS, we must be prepared to stop the Jap when he attempts to kick us.

"Jamieson, I'll ask you to help us out with this show, again. You did well the other day.

"And you, Noble, you'll be a Jap. It's an awful thought but it must be done. Someone has to impersonate evil.

"Now, Noble, face Jamieson.

"Jamieson raise right leg and kick at Noble. That's it, make it real. Give a good kick, as if you were in the chorus.

"Jamieson. Step forward.

"Grab that foot with your left hand a little above the ankle and in back of the heel.

"Lift the foot up high above your own knee. That's it.

"Now grab the toe of her shoe just below the instep with your right hand. Move to your left and try to get behind Noble's body still holding on the leg with both hands as I have indicated.

"No, twist that leg, with both hands, as if you were turning a hammer-handle or a crank.

"You, see, Noble has to fall to the ground.

"What's to be done next?

• "Why, that's simple. You have to keep her on the ground. Just drop to the ground on top of Noble with your right knee bent at the joint and press it right into the small of her back. The fall and the pressure of your knee in her back will keep her there until help will come along, when you can take her captive.

"Is that plain? Good."

WAIST BREACH

"Of course," the Captain said, "all that we have learned is largely for the benefit of our friends, the enemy, bad cess to him. But really, girls," he smiled, "all the wolves are not in civilian life or in the ranks of the enemy."

"Yes," attested Lieut. Martha Schuyler, "there were times on the campus when I could have used a good Judo hold to stop an importunate Big Bad Wolf."

"Well," chuckled the Captain, "you are not too old to learn. I want to demonstrate to you how you can break the hold of a fellow who takes you around the waist."

"Say, Captain," the Lieutenant laughed, "you aren't having any ideas?"

"Suffer the thought. I'm old enough to be your father."

"Oh, oh," she smiled, "feeling fatherly. That's an old gag. I used to have more trouble with the Pater familiars than with the other ambitious goons."

"Be that as it may, Lieutenant, I'll grasp your waist only to show you what you can do to me."

"It'll be a lesson well worth learning."

"All right. I take you around the waist with my right arm. That's, of course, your left side.

"Reach over with your right hand and place the palm of your hand low on my right shoulder. That's right, but hold it firm and rigid.

"Then cover my right arm with your upper-arm at the bicep muscle.

"And now insert your left forearm under my elbow; at the same time, bring up your left hand over and across and grasp your own right wrist, with the knuckles of your hand pointing upward.

"Come on. Now, press my right arm tightly against your left side, holding my arm captive.

"Keep pressing my shoulder back with your right hand and keep lifting your left arm under my imprisoned arm.

"Ouch," he cried, "I feel that. If you put enough pressure on you'll dislocate my shoulder and cause dreadful pain.

"That's it," he said, gritting his teeth. "If I ever had any other designs you would have dissuaded me readily with that hold. Now, please relax. Flesh can stand no more."

"Captain," she said with a twinkle, "I've never done better in all my college career. And I must confess a better man never held me."

This is the complete action:

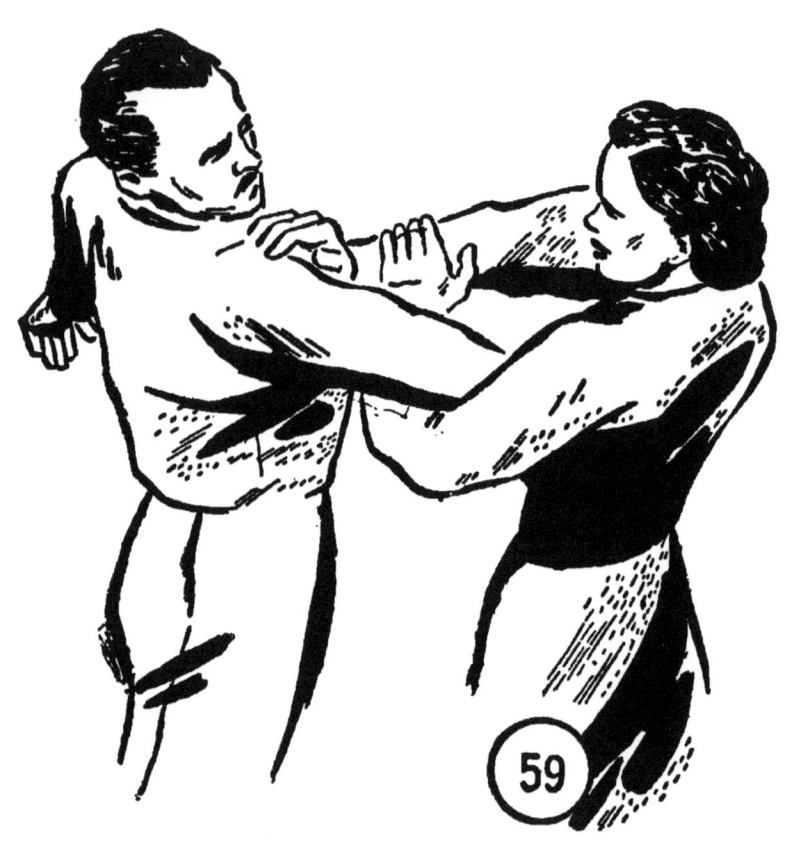

A Selection Of Classic Instructive Titles Relating
To The Art Of Pugilism & Self Defence
In Both War & Peace
Find our entire selection
@ naval-military-press.com

ALL-IN FIGHTING
The distilled knowledge of W.E. Fairbairn, legendary SOE instructor in unarmed combat, and inventor of the Sykes-Fairbairn knife, who learned his deadly skills in 30 years on the Shanghai waterfront. Fully illustrated.
9781847348531

ART OF BOXING AND SCIENCE OF SELF DEFENCE
Former Lightweight Champion Billy Edwards shares the techniques and strategies of the sweet science in his beautifully illustrated boxing guide. Explore boxing's transition from bare knuckle spectacle to today's Marquis of Queensbury ruleset.
9781474539548

SELF DEFENCE OR THE ART OF BOXING
Ned Donnelly was a pioneer of boxing training during the late Victorian era. Explore the strategies and techniques used by this trainer of champions via a series of easy-to-follow illustrations and clear, concise coaching steps.
9781474539562

JACK GOODWIN'S BOXING
This 1920's boxing masterpiece by Jack Goodwin puts you in the shoes of a coach in that era. Uncover the best ways to run, manage and train boxers as taught by Jack Goodwin, a champion and trainer of champions in the noble science.
9781474539586

THE COMPLETE BOXER
Gunner Moir provides detailed instructions on the techniques he deployed to become British Heavyweight Champion. Taught in a series of easy to learn techniques, combinations, and boxing strategies.
9781474539609

ART OF WRESTLING
George de Relwyskow Army Gymnastic Staff

In the appreciation to this book Captain Daniels, V.C., M.C., Rifle Brigade, states: "In adding a word to this book on the style of wrestling as taught at the Headquarters Gymnasium of the British Army, and having had personal experience in the various holds and throws taught, I consider it has been of great value in the training of the soldier, and the bringing out of those qualities of grit and determination which have been seen in all ranks who have taken an active part throughout the greatest war in history." 1919.

9781783313563

KILL OR GET KILLED

Rex Applegate's "kill or be killed" helped prepare America's marines, soldiers, sailors, spies and airmen for the realities of war. This highly shared and respected work provides all you need to know about unarmed combat and close quarter engagement with the enemy.

9781474539661

BOXING (V-Five)
The Aviation Training Office of the Chief of Naval Operations
The game-changing V-Five suite of training manuals helped get a generation of American aviators fit for war. Here we explore how the airmen of the US navy trained in boxing as part of their military fitness regime.
9781474539623

THE TEXTBOOK OF WRESTLING
Get your wrestling skills matt-ready from wrestling champion and world-renown trainer Ernest Gruhn. Replete with detailed holds, throws, pins and strategies for success in a wide range of wrestling rulesets.
9781474539647

MANUAL OF PHYSICAL TRAINING 1914
(United States Army)
Published just prior to the outbreak of World War 1, this beautifully illustrated guide was designed to revolutionise the combat fitness and readiness of the US Army covering a wide range of gymnastic and combat calisthenic exercises.
9781474539708

DEAL THE FIRST DEADLY BLOW
United States Department of the Army
This Vietnam-era classic showcases in detail how the US Forces trained in close quarter combat. Known as the "encyclopaedia of combat" it helped a generation learn how to become devastating effective with empty hands, knives and bayonets alike.
9781474539722

HAND-TO-HAND COMBAT
Bureau of Aeronautics U.S Navy 1943

This is one of the best combative manuals from World War 2, developed by the US Navy V-Five Staff, that included the renowned American wrestler Wesley Brown. It is then not especially surprising that wrestling skills predominate in this manual, and form the base skill-set for this combative system.

9781474537391

ABWEHR ENGLISCHER GANGSTER METHODEN DEFENSE OF ENGLISH GANGSTERS METHODS – SILENT KILLING – FULL ENGLISH TRANSLATION

In 1942 the Wehrmacht published a training manual with the goal of countering the "silent killing" tactics used by the British commando units. The manual was – much in line with typical National Socialist terminology –titled "Abwehr Englischer Gangster-methoden" or "Defence Against English Gangster methods".

This book was compiled due the Wehrmacht intelligence operatives uncovering of a British hand-to-hand course for the SOE, Commandos, et al, on methods of quick and silent killing (undoubtedly developed by W. E. Fairbairn and E. A. Sykes). They correctly assessed that their troops in general and particularly the Geheime Staatspolizei (Gestapo), Sicherheitsdienst (SD), their security guards, and sentries would be in grave danger when confronted by men trained in these methods. This manual/program was the Wehrmacht's response.

9781474538336

BOXING FOR BOYS
Regtl. Sergt.-Major E B Dent Army Gymnastic Headquarters

A successful system of boxing instruction for large classes, to allow tuition with no detriment to the "backward or shy pupil". Covers Kit-On, Guard-Sparring-Advance-Point & Mark-Ducking-Medicine, Bag-Left & Right Hooks etc. The author considered that boxing systematically taught to the youth was beneficial exercise, and would have a marked elevating influence on the national character.

9781783314607

HAND-TO-HAND FIGHTING
A System Of Personal Defence For The Soldier (1918)

A tough book on the art of hand to hand fighting in the trenches of the Great War. Demonstrating techniques utilised to "do away with the enemy", many of which are barred in clean wrestling, the book includes good clear photographic illustrations presenting important attack methods including the "Hammer Lock", "Kidney Kick", "Head Twist", "Knee Groin Kick", and the "Knee Break", all very important in a man to man, life or death encounter, when fighting in the mud of the trenches.

9781783313983

HAND TO HAND COMBAT

Francois d'Eliscu taught thousands of U.S. Army Rangers how to fight down and dirty in World War II. d'Eliscu doesn't get the press that Fairbairn and Applegate do, but he did a commendable job writing this book. It is basic, meant for training raw recruits in a short amount of time before sending them to the front, but simple is good when you are in combat, as most combative experts' will tell you.

9781474535823

COLD STEEL

A cold-war combatives classic. John Styers, US Marine and WW2 veteran, lays out his approach to close quarters combat with rifle, bayonet, stick, knife and empty hands. Explore what helped wartime and post-war Marines stay ahead of the competition with lucid imagery and clear combative descriptions.

9781474540643

THE COMPLETE KANO JIU-JITSU

Join world-famous physical culture expert H. Irving Hancock, and Jiu-Jitsu specialist Katsukama Higashi as they showcase the art of 'Kano Jiu-Jitsu' now known as Judo. Get an exclusive glimpse into the transitional era of the martial art, alongside how it uses Japanese physical culture methodologies for self-improvement.

9781474540735

W.E Fairbairn's Complete Compendium of Lethal, Unarmed, Hand-to-Hand Combat Methods and Fighting In Colour

All 844 images of Fairbairn and his assistants can now for the first time be seen in full colour, lending a clarity to the practical methods of mastering the manner of dealing with an assailant, both in time of war and when placed in difficulty during unpleasant modern urban situations. These various holds, trips, kicks, blows etc. allow the average man or woman a position of security against almost any form of armed or unarmed attack. Captain W.E. Fairbairn would have approved of this new colour version, that gives an illustrative clarity to the original that was lacking in previous monochrome reprints of his work.

All six of W.E. Fairbairn's works in one binding to create the ultimate colour compendium: Get Tough-All-In Fighting-Shooting to Live-Scientific Self-Defence-Hands Off!-Defend
9781783318735

SELF DEFENCE FOR WOMEN COMBATO

Join the Canadian combatives legend William "Bill" Underwood as he showcases self-defence for women. Over the course of clear photography, sketches and instructions he lays out a curriculum for self-defence for the attacks women would be most likely to face.
9781474540711

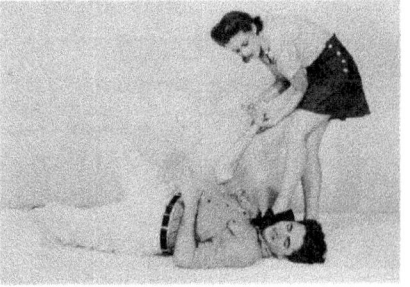

SCIENTIFIC UNARMED COMBAT
The Art of Dynamic Self-Defence

Learn the esoteric Sri Lankan art of 'Cheena-Adi' with R. A Vairamuttu. This guide explores armed and unarmed self-defence drawing heavily from Indian martial culture, alongside wellness and development from Indian physical culture, fitness, diet and medicine.

9781474540728

THE NEW SCIENCE
Weaponless Defence

Join wrestling champions Prof F. S Lewis, William V Gregory and Boxing Champ Tommy Burns as they showcase street orientated self-defence from people with a proven track record of fighting success. This 1906 manual via a series of photos and instructions lays out simple, tried and tested ways to keep yourself safe.

9781474540704

COMBAT CONDITIONING MANUAL
Jiu-Jitsu Defence, Bayonet Defence and Club Defence

This 1942 guide for marines lays out the basics of combat Ju Jitsu as part of an overall training regimen for US Marines. It's a holistic guide that covers defences against armed and unarmed attackers, physical fitness and even first aid.

9781474540698

BOXING TAUGHT THROUGH "SLOW MOTION FILM"

Learn the ropes from the best fighters of the 1900s-1930s in this unique boxing manual. Using stills from super slow-mo fight footage, this treasure trove unpacks the skills, tips and tactics of the champs for you to emulate at home.

9781474540681

HOW TO BOX CORRECTLY

Explore the art of boxing according to famous Bronx boxing brand Ben Lee in this 1944 how-to guide. Learn the ropes from one of the nation's top trainers and boxing journalists John J. Romano, in this warmly illustrated guide to the sweet science.

9781474540674

THE ART OF IN-FIGHTING BY FRANK KLAUS

German-American Middleweight Champ Frank Klaus showcases his KO-scoring boxing IQ in this 1913 guide. Containing clear and easy to understand photography and descriptions, Klaus gives us an insight into the emerging hard-hitting American style of professional boxing.

9781474541473

THE ART OF BOXING AND HINTS ON TRAINING

Crafted just after WW1 in 1919, this guide by Royal Naval Physical Training, Chief Staff Instructor J.O'Neil explores the military benefits of boxing. Showcasing via lucid text and full page photography.

9781474541510

JIM DRISCOLL'S TEXTBOOK OF BOXING

Driscoll was a former Featherweight World Champion and in this 1914 guide, he uses cutting edge and clear photography to showcase the new scientific boxing method. Driscoll showcases to the audience the way to best combine British and American boxing training and fighting philosophy.

9781474541466

JUDO AND ITS USE IN HAND TO HAND COMBAT FROM SEABEES NAVAL ENGINEERING CORPS

Brought to you by William Caldwell of the Seabees Naval Engineering Corps. This WW2 close combat classic provides an insight into the "Combat Judo" used by the navy to prepare personnel for the dangers of theatre. Fully photographed and accessible with clear instructional content to follow.

9781474541480

HAND TO HAND COMBAT - Field Manual 21-150

An example of Cold War / Korean War close combat training. Filled with instructor notes and clear imagery covering unarmed and "cold weapon" combat such as bayonet, knife and garrotte.

9781474541459

AMERICAN JUDO ILLUSTRATED
Brought to you by William Caldwell of the Seabees Naval Engineering Corps. This WW2 close combat classic provides an insight into the "Combat Judo" used by the navy to prepare personnel for the dangers of theatre. Fully photographed and accessible with clear instructional content to follow.
9781474541527

BOXING
This 1906 guide from former English Heavyweight Champion Captain Johnstone, showcases the leading techniques, skills, strategies and fighting philosophies of the day. Brought to life with vivid storytelling from military boxing advocates alongside lucid photography and crisp follow-along guidance for boxers to follow.
9781474541534

KILL OR GET KILLED
Lt Col. Rex Applegate's WW2 Combat Classic 'Kill or Get Killed' is one of the most detailed and comprehensive guides of armed and unarmed combat ever written. From unarmed, to knife, bayonet, pistol, garotte and more – Applegate provides written descriptions, photographs, illustrations on more to showcase and share the skills of forces like the O.S.S.
9781474541541

BALL PUNCHING - A PICTORIAL GUIDE TO THE SPEEDBAG
This 1922 guide from Tom Carpenter is a response to the 'speedbag' craze of the early part of the century. It showcases via clear instructions and photography how to best use tools such as maize, speed and double-end bags for fitness and fighting skills.
9781474541503

SCIENTIFIC BOXING FROM A FISTIC EXPERT
Diet - Fight Training - K.O. Punching
This 1937 guide to the American school and style of professional boxing provides a clear and well-illustrated suite of technical skills and drills to compete successfully. Replete with training advice, rule guidance and ring Generalship principles to help boxers be inline with the latest advice and training acumen.
9781474541497

www.ingramcontent.com/pod-product-compliance
Lightning Source LLC
LaVergne TN
LVHW010318070426
835510LV00031B/3448